I dedicate this book to all creative and curious children who explore the world with their crayons and imagination. May these colorful pages inspire joy, a love of nature, and endless hours of artistic fun. May each stroke be a celebration of the magic that lives within each little artist. May this book bring smiles and special moments to all who read it. With affection,
Michel

Luiz Michel Vargas da Silva
2024

This Book Belongs to:

____

Test Color Page

VE PO CIU WJ

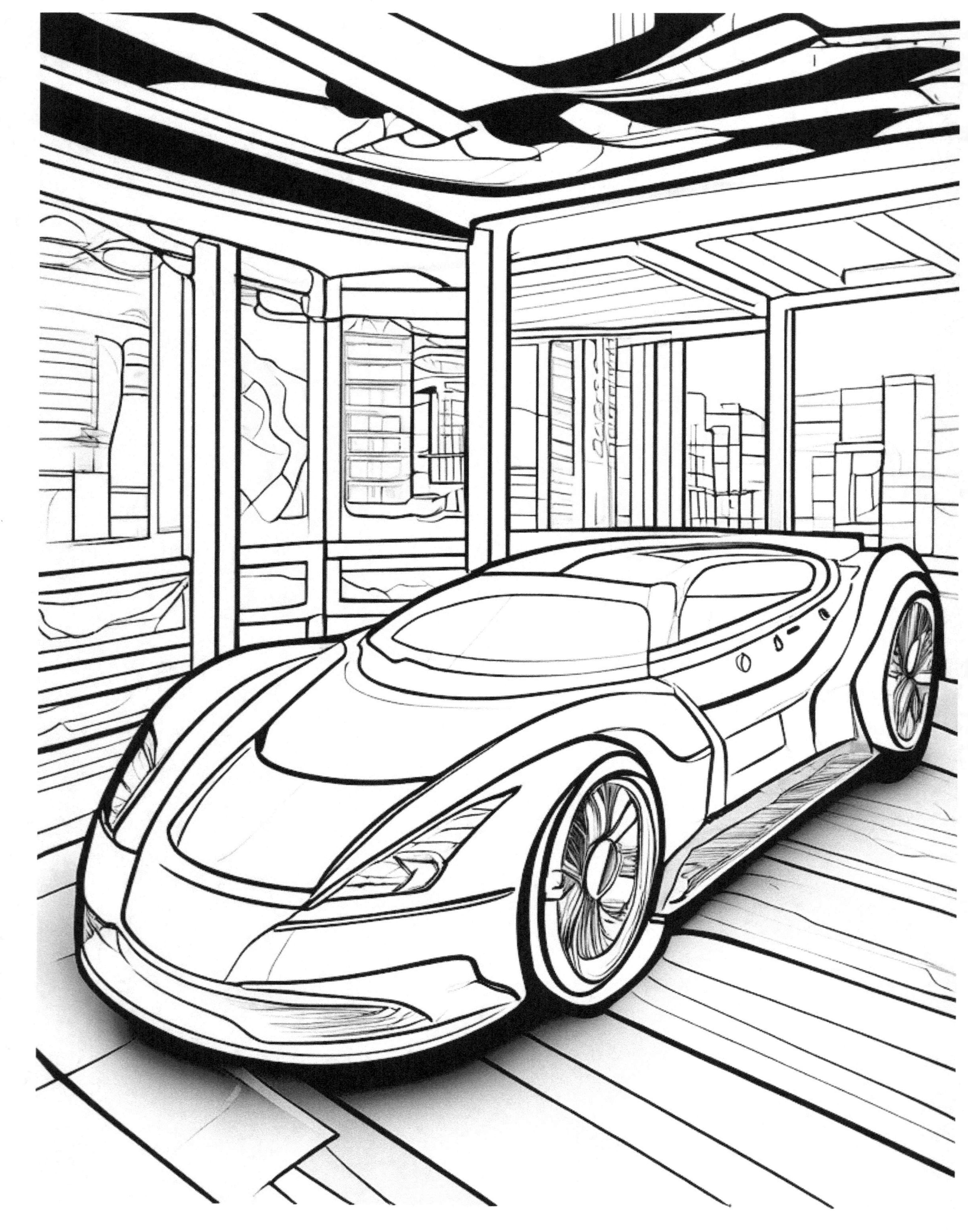

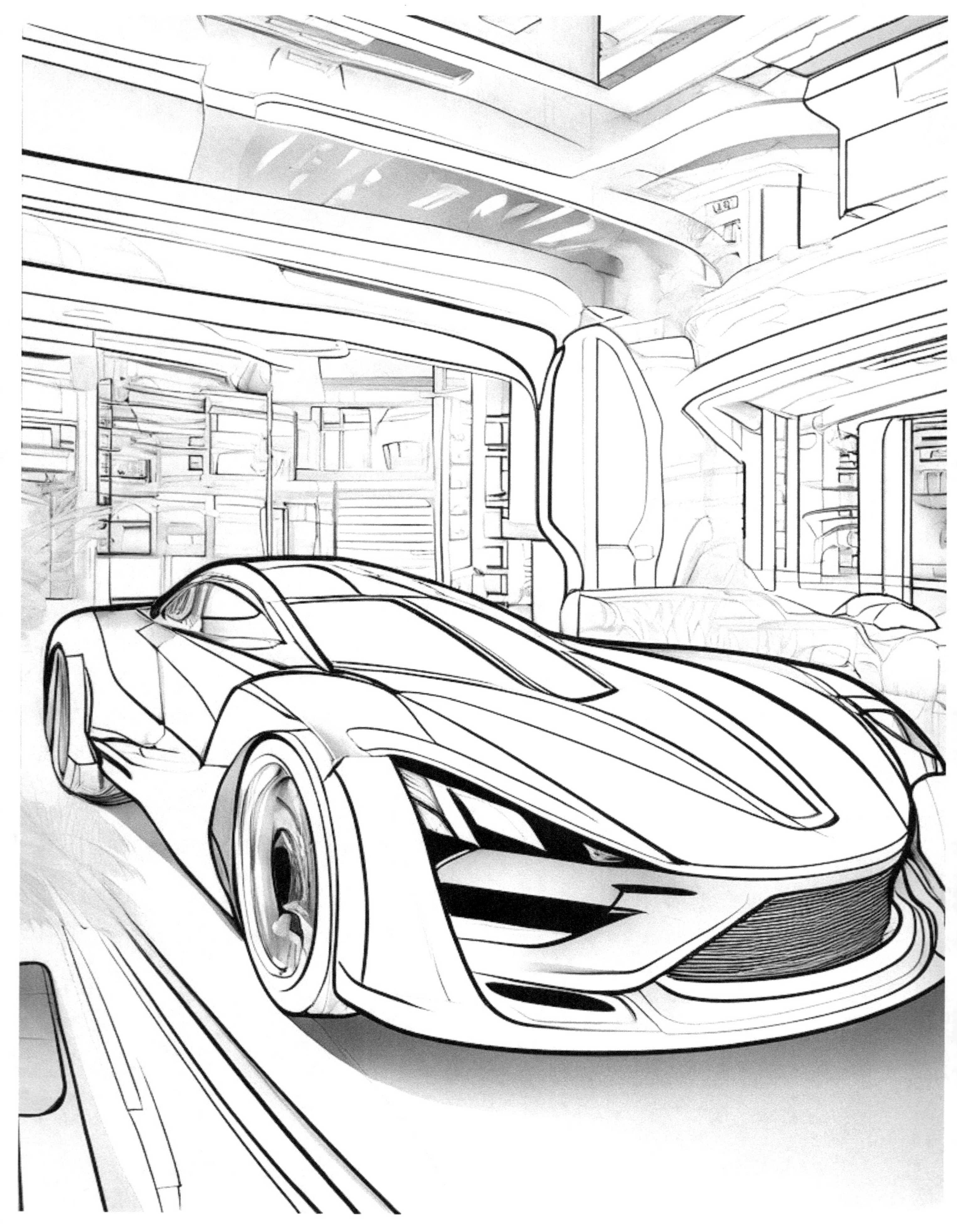